EMBRACING NEXT

An Empty Nest Enjoyment Guide

Enjoy!
Love,
Kim

WRITTEN BY KIM SMITH

An Unbelievable Freedom Book

Being a mother redefines us, reinvents us,
destroys and rebuilds us.

SHONDA RHIMES

DEDICATION

This book is dedicated to mothers, especially two.

The first is my own beloved mother, Eleanor.
Thank you for always being there, Mum.

The second is my friend Vicki, whose children grew up alongside my own. I admired her as a devoted mother, and I know her memory lives on through those whose lives she touched.

Vicki Ann Lynch, 1973-2019

Table of Contents

Welcome from Kim

This is the space in the book where, as the workbooks have become a series, I've chosen to say a bit about why I included the author and the topic. Why I have chosen the author is completely obvious. I'm a big fan, and I have unlimited access to her!

As for the topic of the empty nest transition, it's such an important time in a woman's life. It's also the one I'm living through right now. I've been an "empty nester" for 14 months, and they've been dynamic ones. As for books already written on the empty nest, from my perspective, many are overly sentimental and self-indulgent. Other are super sarcastic and snarky. This book offers MY thoughts on how to thrive during this period of upheaval. No matter your emotional style, you'll admit the empty nest is a renegotiation of what a woman has known for 18, 20, 25, even 30 years. Such a time brings challenges and opportunities.

I've written about my issues growing up, marriage, career challenges, and my battle with weight. Until now, I have not written about my children. Part of this was for their privacy, but it's also because I wasn't ready. Raising them is the most powerful and transformative thing I've done, and speaking about the journey, even looking directly at it, feels tender. But as I'm about to describe in these pages, those feelings shouldn't be numbed or avoided. We should face them and flow with them.

My children are currently 23 and 20 years old, in the same stage of their lives that I was in when they were born. What was mothering them from a young age like? As motherhood is at any age, it was a beautifully mixed blessing.

It gave me a pure sense of purpose that drove my identity. Knowing they needed me created a reason for being, a feeling of safety, a deeply secure groundedness. At times, it also felt like suffocation, like stifling boredom when I wanted freedom. It often felt like I'd lost myself before I ever really found myself.

But the joy and delight they infused into my days, for that I'll always be grateful. I recall moments of transcendent awe, looking at their beautiful faces and knowing I made them. My love for them, well, if you're a mother, I don't have to tell you how all-consuming it is. It's a love that inspires and impels, and as your children move on, there are other channels ready to receive some of what you've been pouring into them. That's what this book is all about.

Enjoy Your Life,
Kim

Introduction

The Nest as a Metaphor

It's now obvious to me, sitting in the center of my "empty nest", why all the imagery of welcoming and raising children centers on birds. Birds parent in a tidy, efficient way that's easier to describe than the equivalent human endeavor.

First, there is the busy phase of preparation: feathering the nest so it can be filled. We even refer to human mothers as "nesting" when the instinctual drive to prepare a space for a new baby kicks in. Then comes the phase that I call being in the trenches, the one where the children so completely fill your home and life that there's scarcely space for anything else.

Every modern parent trying to raise children properly while carving out space for themselves knows this balancing act. It's like teetering on the very edge, threatening to fall out of the tree because the nest is so crowded by the kids and their trappings.

Unlike birds, we get to practice by letting our children to go to school, to visit family and friends, to overnight camps and other trials of being apart. We start to realize that we can survive without them and they without us, but the question nags, how will it be when this is the permanent reality?

And of course, the day comes for the children to leave the family nest. They spread their metaphorical wings, flap them vigorously, and then fly! Some have a rough, bumpy start, falling to the ground instead of the air. They need to come back to the nest and wait a bit longer before they try again, which triggers a jumble of emotions, I'm sure.

Others immediately soar higher and higher, out of sight in what seems like a breath, leaving behind a different but equally complicated set of feelings: pride and joy, grief and loss.

At times, the emotional paradox creates the same crowding as the children physically caused, feelings pushing and shoving against each other like elbows and knees. This is what makes our journeys as parents so different from the well-defined cycles our avian friends enjoy.

We Aren't Birds

For birds, it's straightforward. For us, not so much. In modern human society, we don't get the clear-cut set of instinctual instructions that program birds. We do not lay and hatch eggs, feed and fledge babies, then do it all again the following spring.

I don't pretend to speak for the emotional experience of birds or any animal - but I suspect they avoid big tangles of regrets over their mistakes. There may have been a day when they didn't return with enough worms to feed everyone equally, but they probably aren't still beating themselves up about it.

We are hard-wired differently than other animals. We have memories, good and bad, and we have stories we tell ourselves about how things went down, what we COULD have done better, and what we WOULD have done well, given more time, energy, money, etc. It's important to handle these regrets carefully if we want to move forward in a wholehearted way. This book offers a framework for shifting perspectives on what *was*, so we can thrive in what *is*.

The key to flourishing beyond the empty nest lies in intentionally shifting these perspectives. This requires vigilant attentiveness to our thoughts and feelings. By intentionally sculpting an overarching narrative of parenting as positive, we can move forward. We can view it as something we did the best that we could. We can take pride of achievement in the parts that were smooth, and carry faith that the rough parts taught deeper lessons for us and the kids. It's not about denial or rewriting history, but about gently reframing and refocusing. This is the best way to support freedom for all involved.

Flight Patterns Abound

Unlike birds, who have one batch of eggs each season, then stop automatically when no longer of reproductive age, there are dozens of ways to be a human parent. There are so many different styles and approaches. You can start "early" or "late." You can have one child - or two - or ten. You can have the children quite closely spaced, or spread so far apart that it's almost a complete starting-all-over-again. Sometimes an adopted child or stepchild comes into the mix that disrupts the birth order and dynamics of the sibling group. You can welcome the children according to a well-designed plan, by surprise, or through a mixture of both.

My experience wasn't particularly unusual. I got a fairly early start - I was 22 when I gave birth to my son, then I had my daughter 3 years later at age 25. Having a boy, then a girl meant I never heard anyone ask when I was going to "try again" for the opposite. Very few escape that level of scrutiny, but I was grateful that I did.

Most notable about my parenting was that the kids' father and I divorced when they were ages 5 & 2, and I raised them in a shared-custody arrangement from that point on. Sharing custody had a major impact on me and on them, of course, but the point of this book is the empty nest. Navigating the empty nest has its own challenges no matter how things go down during the parenting years.

I became an empty nester just before my 45th birthday, and it was my son, the oldest, who moved out last, not first. I'd always known the empty nest would likely arrive in my 40s. I had deeply dreaded it when I wasn't beckoning it, but either way, the moment arrived. He was settled in his first apartment, she was away at college, their childhood bedrooms were empty, and I was emotionally jolted. They had been my structure, my purpose, my entertainment, and my constant companions, and now that chapter was closed.

You may not be able to pinpoint a defining moment when your empty nest happened. If you have one child who moves out and is independent from that day forward, it's a particular day you'll remember forever. For those with larger families or unique circumstances, there may not have been such a clear-cut point. The word "boomerang" is used to describe the pattern of young adult children moving in and out as life circumstances change. No matter what, you know when you started to feel a shift and recognized that the active Momming phase had run its course.

Maybe the transition was a really simple one for you. If so, congratulations! I suspect many who choose to pick this book up had an experience with a few more layers, and I hope the perspective in the pages ahead will support your process.

What's Next (In This Book)

A few words about how this book is structured before you turn the page and begin. The book is organized into three sections: **Reframe**, **Refocus** and **Refeather**.

Reframing is a technique for shifting your lens and looking at a set of circumstances with an open mind and heart. It's about being more flexible and generous with your interpretation of yourself, others, and events. The first part of the book will deal with emotions and reframing them.

Refocusing is about reallocating our energy and time. It's about gathering up the bandwidth that was distributed to the children and their needs and placing it onto the people and activities that best support us enjoying our lives moving forward.

Refeather is a made-up word. Birds "feather" their nests by building them out of leaves, sticks, and yes, their own feathers. We are going to "refeather" our nests by using the emptiness as a canvas for building toward what we want and who we want to be.

An Empty Nest Inventory

Before we begin, let's look back on the motherhood journey. This book involves reflecting on many memories, so let's get grounded.

At what age did you first become a mother?

Was it planned, or was it a surprise?

Have you experienced the phenomenon known as 'the empty nest'?

If yes, how long ago?

What do you miss the most about actively taking care of your child(ren)?

What do you miss the least?

What is the story you tell yourself about the job you did as a mother?

Is that story one you are open to rewriting with a new twist?

OK, turn the page and let's embrace what's next!

PART ONE

Reframe

Reframing an Unacknowledged Milestone into a Revered Rite-of-Passage

I think one of the hardest parts of becoming an empty nester is that it usually passes unacknowledged. There is no ceremonial rite of passage associated with it. When you discover that a child will enter your life, your family gathers around. The community, on some level, is delighted by the news that a new baby is on the way.

This may not be as solid as in generations past; our modern lives are geographically spread and time-and-energy strapped. However, traditions persist such as happy announcements, baby showers, and the giving of gifts. The mother-to-be is made to feel supported and special at this important moment of transition in her life.

The last child leaving home creates no equivalent fuss. The moment is ignored, which sets the stage for "empty nest syndrome," which sounds almost like a medical diagnosis. Maybe in your family, someone took you out to dinner or even on a trip. Maybe you chose to take a day to yourself or a trip to the spa to acknowledge the importance of the change happening in your life. I hope you did, but I know it's just as likely, perhaps even more likely, that the moment passed unacknowledged.

I can't claim that I took myself for a day at the spa to celebrate my empty nest accomplishment - I didn't. But I also have an unusual situation where my first months of empty nesting overlapped with my first months of self-employment, and I've done many self-focused things in that time, most notably traveling alone. Each trip invited self-discovery, and as a series, they became a rite-of-passage in my empty nest journey. It's why I'm leading this book off in this way.

Questions to Ponder

I invite you to reflect on your own empty nest transition, whether it was a week ago, a decade ago, or is still in the future.

Did you have a specific rite of passage ceremony around your empty nest milestone? Describe how it enhanced your experience here.

If you did not have a ceremony of any kind, design one. It can involve other people, but it really doesn't need to. This is for you, so really reflect on what kind of activity or event would create both celebration and closure.

Reframing Heavy Sadness into Purposeful Mourning

The next few reflections are about the purely emotional aspects of the empty nest transition, and they may or may not apply to you. Read and reflect, and if they resonate, proceed to the Reclaim Invitation that accompanies each. I'm starting off with the sadness that can seem to swallow some of us up during the empty nest. I've talked to a few people who said it felt exactly like grieving someone who had died - waves of sudden desolation coming out of nowhere, weeping, feelings of emptiness.

I remember that when our daughter moved into our college dorm (just a few miles up the road, mind you), I went through a brief phase where I mourned the idea that she'd never again be at home with me in the same way. I recall my husband Ryan coming out onto the screen porch that September, finding me sitting with tears streaming down my face. In his typically supportive way, he'd just smile and leave me to it. It was a kind of grieving for sure.

The fact is that there has been a death of sorts, the end of one of life's most meaningful phases. The sadness is understandable and expected, though it's different for each one of us. It can also be sadness or grief over the things that you didn't get a chance to do, for example, a dream you had to travel with your children while they were small or provide certain experiences for them.

I can even let myself feel sad that I never managed to buy the kids matching sets of bedroom furniture. They always had beds, dressers, and everything else they needed, but somehow time got away from me and I never did what I said I would do: buy them real furniture with all matching pieces.

It's OK to feel sad, but the key lies in not letting the sadness be overwhelming and never-ending. Sometimes trying to rationalize the grief, i.e, scolding yourself that no one really died or shaming yourself as being ridiculous, can make things worse. My suggestion in this Reframe is to face the sadness and really allow it to come through. Allow yourself to feel sad, to cry, to look through the baby pictures, or to feel whatever you feel. Just as with any other kind of grief, allow it to wash over you in waves and then recede as it inevitably will.

Then, after being intentional about allowing a space for grieving or mourning, you can put it aside and get back into living. By dealing with the sadness appropriately, you don't have to carry it. You don't have to feel swallowed up by it. It can become a healthy part of preparing for the phase that comes next.

Questions to Ponder

I invite you to honor whatever sadness you have about your days of active motherhood being in the past. You may have minimal sadness, or it may feel like the sadness is encompassing you.

Ask yourself, did you experience any waves of intense sadness about the arrival of the empty nest? How did you honor those feelings?

If you have not taken space for purposeful mourning, it's never too late to do so.

Reframing Nagging Regret into Self Forgiveness

Regrets are normal. Show me the mother who raises a child for 18+ years and looking back, has zero regrets about any of the things she did or didn't do in the process. Ryan is fascinated by Bigfoot and the Loch Ness Monster. That is exactly how I feel about the regret-free mother. Has anyone ever seen one? Was it captured on film somewhere?

Regrets are dangerous, though, and that's why I want to talk about them here. They can become so interwoven with the story we tell about ourselves as mothers that they're almost invisible. We think of our children and a bad feeling comes up, a sad or heavy energy. It might be a nagging "Coulda, shoulda, woulda been a better mother" that's triggered by an unforgiven regret.

So, this reframe is about forgiving yourself. Did you miss an important school or sports event? Do you feel you worked too much? Did you ever lash out in frustration and anger? There was a phase when my son was around 11 when his nighttime anxiety had him (and me!) awake several nights in a row and finally, in sheer exhaustion, I shook him by the shoulders. The clearest part of the memory is that even though he was a child, he was already as tall as I am. I can remember my arms straight out in front of me. I didn't shake him long or hard - but I still feel a wash of shame and regret when I remember it.

I worked extremely hard to never, ever lay hands on my children in frustration or anger. I deplore physical aggression; they weren't even allowed to fight or wrestle as a form of play. More recently, as I'm doing lots of deep self-work, I've forgiven myself for this out-of-character incident.

Is it right to shake an anxious kid struggling with insomnia and bad dreams by the shoulders? No. It's wrong, but it happened. We haven't talked about it in a long time, but I believe my son has forgiven me, and it was finally time to forgive myself and be free. It was an important reminder of how crucial sleep is for me, and the lesson benefited both kids as I became more focused on getting enough rest.

Self-forgiveness takes gentle intention, journaling, reprocessing, and sometimes therapy. I'm learning about the utility of Emotional Freedom Technique ("EFT" or "Tapping") in the process of forgiving yourself, and I'm interested enough that it will be a topic of a future Unbelievable Freedom Habit Guide. Keep an eye out, and in the meantime, do whatever you need to do to forgive and feel free.

Questions to Ponder

I invite you now to examine and explore regret in relation to your motherhood journey.

Do you have deep regrets about something you did or didn't do as a mother?

Are you willing to forgive yourself and let it go for good?

This is deep reflective work. Take some time to consider it, and use the adjacent space to journal about it. Make a self-forgiveness action plan and revisit it as needed.

Reframing Guilty Anticipation into Deep Contentment

Let's talk about another empty-nest emotion that isn't mentioned often: the eager anticipation! No more need to rinse someone else's toothpaste out of the sink or turn inside-out clothing items the proper way to go in the laundry. No more need to nag anyone to get up (or go to bed, or do chores, or homework, or.....) Whatever it may be, there is some aspect of the parenting grind that you most definitely won't miss. You may feel a sense of expansive freedom when you think about leaving those tasks behind.

Isn't giddy glee a good thing? Isn't feeling a sense of excitement about being released from certain chores or routines a positive? Yes, as long as you can frame them in the right light. There is no need to feel guilty, and I know that in this complex emotional swirl, guilt can arise. I've heard about celebrities who have been chastised after admitting in an interview that the empty nest felt like freedom for them. Societal judgment can turn what's already a complicated emotional landscape into a trap.

I've alluded to feeling stifled and bored when the kids were growing up, particularly when they were very little. I didn't enjoy the developmental play that's so important for children - it's actually a gift some mothers have more than others, just like cooking, crafts, etc. Playing with their toys and games made me feel restless. At times when those sentiments were strong, I found myself looking forward to them being older.

Of course, as they grew, they had interests I enjoyed, like building certain collections, and they became interesting conversationalists. The older they got, the more I felt I could engage with them on terms that were comfortable for me and my personality. But I could still let myself feel guilty over the times I was "wishing it away"....and I don't. I don't let myself waste time now about what can't be changed then.

Mom Guilt is real. Maybe you did a superior job rejecting it throughout your child-rearing years, and if so, kudos. Mom guilt is a societal construct that depletes maternal energy, energy that could be far better spent elsewhere. However, it's real enough that it creeps in for most, and it can similarly creep in during our empty nest transition if we aren't mindful.

If you know me and my writing, you knew contentment was going to come into the equation. My quest to fulfill my grandmother's Enjoy-Your-Life legacy brought me to a deep place of contentment, a continuous contentment flow. That is where I want you to channel your feelings of eager anticipation. Channel them into fuel for building a contentment foundation. You are allowed to enjoy the freedom you've earned. You can feel deeply contented to have arrived at this stage of your life. It's not only OK, it's necessary. This is your invitation to reclaim contentment, guilt-free.

Questions to Ponder

Have you noticed moments of eager anticipation of a kid-free future being clouded by guilt?

Identify a specific thing you prefer about your life now vs. when you were raising your kid(s). How can you focus on this aspect in a positive way?

PART TWO

Refocus

Refocusing Hollow Hours into Making Meaning

The transition to the empty nest has been described by some as a "loud quiet", like the quiet that descends after children have clamored out the door to run for the school bus or to hop into a waiting car in the driveway. The slammed door makes its final echoes, the voices fade, and then.....silence. It's so quiet, it's loud in its own way.

Particularly with my daughter, I went through a period of several years where she was my main companion. This was during her late elementary and middle school years. Early on, I'd playfully refer to her as my "truck dog" because anywhere I was going, she was eager to hop in and ride along. We had so many similar interests, coffee and pastries and bargain-hunting. Once she started moving toward the high school stage, I joked that I was her coolest friend because I was the only one who had money and could drive. Kidding aside, she was great built-in company for me, and I had to adjust to her not being there once she got into high school and DID have friends with money and cars.

I never stood in her way, because even though I missed her easy, built-in friendship, I knew it was normal for her to come to prefer the company of her same-age peers almost exclusively. I figured it out, as moms do, and found new ways to spend my time.

For many, the transition to not having children at home frees up so many hours - hours and hours of time. There are no more doctor, dentist and orthodontist appointments...no more nightly homework, math problems, and science fair posters....no more overnight playdates and trips to the mall. This liberates hours in each day, and as they add up, in each week and month.

How are you using them? For some, opportunities abound to fill those hours with hobbies both old and new, friendships both old and new, and activities both old and new. Many have been eagerly awaiting the day they could start painting, writing, knitting or crocheting again. Some were waiting for time to take a dance class or finally learn to play the guitar. It's a revelation that the time has finally arrived.

But for others, it's a genuine challenge to come up with ways to fill the hours. It's fine, especially at first, if the hours are being taken up by so-called mindless pursuits like TV, social media, or even napping. It's all well and good to decompress and spend some true downtime just being. But as time goes on, you want to reclaim these hours. You want to refocus on moving your life in meaningful directions.

This requires a look back to before children, to the things you loved that may have been set aside, or the people who were important but drifted away. Some have kept those relationships fresh throughout, but many will admit that they spent years busy and distracted with raising a family.

Now is the time to do the things that were understandably put on hold. Now is the time to ask yourself how YOU want to spend your hours, with no agenda but your own. Reflect on how you'd like to refocus those hours now.

Questions to Ponder

What is ONE activity, hobby or pastime that you allowed to slide off the radar during the years you were juggling family responsibilities? Does it hold interest for you anymore?

What is ONE friendship or relationship that drifted apart while your children were growing up? Is there any chance of reviving it now?

Refocusing Bygone Routines into Meaningful Rituals

Part of my intentional contentment practice is a habit I call Everyday Rituals, bringing slow and mindful energy to the small patterns of our daily lives. The only difference between an everyday ritual and going-through-the-motions is intention. Maybe you had daily rituals with your children when they were growing, and if so, that's wonderful. But for many of us, the hustle and bustle of school and schedules causes a bit of mindful intention to get lost.

An unusual fact about me is that I love doing laundry. I always found the sounds and smells of clean laundry very meditative, and I enjoyed folding the children's clothing and stacking it in little piles. It was certainly a kind of ritual for me. There were many more chores (cooking for picky eaters, cleaning the kitchen, washing floors) that I disliked, and I did them mindlessly. Now they need doing far less often. Regardless of how you felt about your routines, the shift is something you can harness for creating rituals.

There's nothing wrong with having standard routines, and my children's presence imposed a structure I needed to power through my days. But once they grew up, in their absence I saw an opportunity to create new everyday rituals, and I've done just that.

I've heard the departure of children's busy routines referred to as "loud quiet." The quiet can be strange as we adjust in a space previously filled with noise. Even the happy noise of laughter, playing, and slamming doors creates distraction, and now those distractions are extinguished. So what to do with this new space, this hard-earned silence?

Create new rituals that have meaning for you. Maybe they're totally self-focused ones. In my book *Poster Girl for Contentment*, which describes my full contentment practice, I talk about taking yourself on a date, and my main example is my latte ritual. That's just one of dozens of ways to spend time with yourself, looking within and asking the questions about where you want life to flow next. The answers are there, and they'll emerge if you create the circumstances for them to drift up in.

You can also form new rituals with your young adult children, especially if they are local. Maybe they aren't around at mealtime every night, but you could develop a new ritual of Sunday dinner or some kind of monthly outing to a restaurant. The balance of how much to just let them live their lives and how much to attempt to "draw them back in" is a delicate one, and one I'm working to strike now. But the blank canvas of the empty nest is a definite opportunity for new rituals.

Questions to Ponder

If there are bygone rituals you had when your children were growing, what do you miss most about them?

What do you miss least?

How could you bring back the spirit of what you loved most about those days?

Refocusing a Juggling Act into Focused Freedom

Being a mother and career woman is a primary example of role strain: a state of being in which the competing demands of two roles constantly clash. Still, there are tons of women finding a blend of both roles and I'm not here to say it can't be done. I'm here to say that once the child-rearing part of life is done, there's a large amount of bandwidth to be reclaimed and rechanneled into your career of choice.

This applies even if you have not been working outside the home for the past few years - or ever. You still have a sudden influx of bandwidth that can be channeled into a pursuit that's just for you. Whether it be professional, creative, or some blend of the two, now is the time.

Erik Erikson called the developmental stage of partnering, parenting and family "Intimacy vs. Isolation" and most charts have it labeled from ages 21-39 (we have to expand our thinking a little bit in this day and age). However, he went on to call the following stage, often labeled ages 40-65, "Generativity vs. Stagnation." What that meant is that the years that follow the ones spent focused on family are the ones where you are "generative", or creating a body of work as a legacy beyond family.

This should not feel like pressure. You don't have to go paint a Mona Lisa. It's simply an invitation to step back and get intentional about your career. Maybe you've been waiting for this day for so long, and now that it's here, it's overwhelming. Perhaps you told yourself that you'd pursue a promotion or go back to school when the kids grew up, and they did! You finally have the attention and energy you've been wanting - and it's daunting!

Breathe. Tension and resistance are the enemies of flowing forward. What do you *want*? This is a huge exploration to make, in terms of the empty nest or any context. It brings up big questions about the meaning of our lives and the purpose of our existences. I invite you to see it as exhilarating! If you already do, let that build. If you aren't there, make a little space for excitement to weave itself into your current story.

Questions to Ponder

If you've been working all along, how can the next career phase be better than the last because of renewed focus?

What have you always wanted to do in your career but felt you lacked enough bandwidth?

If it's time for an entirely new career or new venture, what's one concrete step you can take toward it now?

PART THREE

Refeather

Refeathering Vacant Spaces into Fresh Foundations

The departure of the children is a transition for the home space itself, too. The biggest empty-nest cliche of all is what to do with the childhood bedrooms. Leave them untouched like shrines? Strip them down a bit to serve as guest bedrooms, put in a home gym, create an office or craft room? I'm here to give you the right answer....

There isn't one. It is not wrong to keep your child's room as it looked when occupied, with their childhood things adorning the walls. It's not wrong to give the room a facelift. It's not wrong to get rid of all that stuff and turn it into something you've always wanted. This is the spirit of the entire perspective shift this book is trying to encourage: there is no right or wrong, only what supports your flow.

In fact, you may be thinking or feeling that it's time to fly away from this nest and take up residence in a new one. That's no problem, either. I feel a growing desire to move into a tiny house with stained glass windows and lots of cozy features. We are heading into Maine winter as I write this, but next spring, we'll see where that urge takes me.

Thoughts may rise up about how your kids need a familiar nest to return to, but this is about what's best for you. If you're feeling a stirring, even a faint urge to move on, listen to it and see where it leads. The home you occupy for the next chapter may very well be the one you've been in (my Gram lived in her house 66 years, through the raising of her children, grandchildren, AND great-grandchildren) but it also may not. Whatever feels right for you is the right answer.

Questions to Ponder

What feelings come up when you think about rearranging or redecorating your child's former bedroom?

How about when you envision selling your house or moving on to a new rental?

Picture what was a "dream home" a few years ago, when you might have inhabited it with children in tow. Is it the same now, or is it different?

Refeathering a Co-Parenting Relationship into a True Partnership

If you have a partner in your life, do you remember what your life together was like before the children came along? Invariably, you had different interests back then than you have now. Presumably the central focus for your life together was, well,.....your life together. It was likely not kid-centric in the beginning. As for me, my husband Ryan and I met when my children were ages 7 and 4. I was sharing custody of them, but they were with me about 80% of the time, so our early relationship contained only a modicum of kid-free time (and they were never far from my thoughts.)

As such, our life as partners who are not co-parenting is just beginning. What a revelation it feels like to remember ourselves before "the kids." And though they're still on the periphery, we are learning to go days at a time without talking about them, what they're doing or what they might need. Yes, we've let our 13-year old beagle slip into a stereotype, treating him as a sort of spoiled youngest child, but he never interrupts our conversations.

The advice gets repeated, act like you're dating. I'd say that it is advice we are taking, trying to be intentional about making plans to spend time together and minimize other distractions. We've both thrown ourselves into creative projects (you know, like me typing a workbook right now rather than spending the day with him) but it's done with a sense of intention and mutual respect for one another.

I do as much to support his writing as I would if I were a new girlfriend instead of a wife of 16 years. That is the spirit of it. It isn't just about sending flowers or buying gifts. It's a renewed focus on the other person as a unique individual who is also still growing and developing.

It's also a research-proven fact that the best way to keep a relationship fresh is to involve novelty. The reason people in new relationships fall into quick intimacy bolstered by plenty of erotic feelings is in that three-letter word: new. Also, I'm typing this workbook in a coffeehouse where a fussy toddler is loudly wailing. I haven't met the person who considers that noise a turn-on and if they exist, I don't want to meet them!

If despite best efforts, another truth is emerging - that without being co-parents, there's nothing left to carry forward - know that it's OK to make separating part of the refeathering process. The decision is a huge, life-altering one, and not one I expect anyone to make because of a self-improvement workbook, but I mention it here because it's important.

Another of my Poster Girl Habits is Editing, or empowered willingness to make big life changes, and that's the biggest one of all. Just know that if thriving in the empty nest means being single or "self partnered" for a while, that is a part of the journey that you can flow through, too.

Questions to Ponder

When you think back on life before children, what did you enjoy most about the partner or relationship in your life at that time?

If you're still with the same partner, can you think of ways to invite some of that back?

If you're with someone new, how can you bring a fresh element to the relationship since the kids departed?

If you're in a situation that needs to change (single but don't want to be, or in a relationship that feels wrong), think about how you might take the next step to move toward where you want to be.

Refeathering a Retired Role to an Invigorated Identity

I've read other books on the empty nest where the author confessed that their central identity was as "So and So's mother." My children have their father's last name, an uncommon one. My current married name is Smith, so I was occasionally mistaken as the mother of a classmate with the oh-so-common name Smith. For this reason, rather than being called Mrs. Smith, I preferred teachers to refer to me as Adam & Emma's mom.

As much as I love my kids, and still love being "Adam and Emma's Mom," I don't think my whole identity was built around it. I was always in an intense pursuit of my purpose and identity as an individual, which caused its own struggles that I've documented in other writing.

Still, I can see how a mother, especially one who raised several children now grown and flown might wake up asking herself, Who am I, anyway? It's also been described as, suddenly finding yourself at the center of your own life. Isn't that a lovely image, waking up at the center of your life? Even typing the words is exciting to me, which says that my empty nest transition is a fairly successful one.

I encourage empty nest mothers to tap into a kind of creativity that may feel new: the energy of self-creation. You may not think you're creative, but you're creating yourself each day. The process of "self improvement" is just a way to actively dig into self creation. You can go to therapy, read books, take classes, or do things like buy a self-improvement type workbook. In fact, since you're reading this, I don't need to go any further into explaining that concept. Work on yourself! Enjoy that process!

Focus on the image of your ideal health and happiness. You know where you've been and who you've been until now. A critical aspect of refeathering your nest and your life is deciding who you'll be going forward.

Questions to Ponder

If empty nest was in the past, do you recall that feeling of lost identity once you weren't called "So and So's mom" anymore? Or did it feel liberating?

What about the imagine of waking up at the center of your own life, does that resonate?

Write about where the center of your life is right now, and whether it is someplace you definitely want to be.

Refeathering an Ending into a Beginning

At this point, I've suggested that you make ten perspective shifts. Some may have been needed, while others didn't fit your situation at all. In any event, here is the 11th and final shift I'll suggest for enhanced enjoyment of your empty nest experience.

Repeat after me: Life is not over.

Maybe you never thought that life would be over at the empty nest. I hope you didn't; it's a terrible limiting belief to hold. I'm coming at this book (as I do with all my writing) from the perspective of what I've lived, and during my most mired years, I thought those exact words. My children gave me a strong sense of purpose when I couldn't see it elsewhere, so I feared and dreaded the day when they were grown.

Like salt in a wound, I'd tell myself that once they didn't need me, I'd have no purpose because I hadn't attained any status or standing in the world. Thinking that way led me to a state of despair. I'm so grateful that I moved beyond that mire, because despair is hopeless, and without hope, you cannot move.

Because of the work I've done over the past six years in pursuit of my grandmother's Enjoy-Your-Life message, when my empty nest moment arrived, I was happily busy with many things. We'd just published *Unbelievable Freedom*, the intermittent fasting memoir that started my writing career, so the same weekend my son was moving out, positive feedback about the book was pouring in.

Over the 14 months since, I've gone into a turbo-mode of personal growth and development, and I've done a lot of soul searching and introspection. I spend time almost every day alone in nature. I've traveled by car and by plane, around the region and across the country, to see new cities and spend time with new friends.

As a self-employed person, I've chosen pursuits that follows my curiosity, so I've spent my work time doing tasks I enjoy. My days are spent engrossed in projects I find energizing and enlivening. I've given talks on my books, taught workshops, and attended conferences.

If you had told me six years ago that both kids would be out on their own, happy and healthy, and that I'd be doing the things I've done over this year, I wouldn't have believed it. It's truly Unbelievable Freedom to live with so much health and happiness.

It was the pursuit of enjoying my life that taught me all my lessons, and shown me that my best years are just beginning. Coming to believe that I could enjoy a moment turned into enjoying a day, which turned into enjoying weeks and months and years. That's what it's really about, stringing moments into days and then into a lifetime.

You too can carve out a life that includes all that matters most to you: space for yourself, space for your grown children, space for your partner, space for your career, hobbies, and friendships. Eventually, if you're as lucky as my grandmother, you'll be 95 years old, wonderful and wise, giving your own granddaughter an Enjoy Your Life blessing.

Questions to Ponder

Can you relate to the idea of life ending after the active years of motherhood? Or did you always know it was only the end of one chapter?

What feelings drift up when you hear the words "turbo mode of personal development" (how I describe the past year of my life)?

What is ONE thing happening in your world right now that serves as a symbol of a new life beginning?

Concluding Sentiments

If you picked this book up with heaviness in your heart about your empty nest, I hope you've felt a tangible shift. It's my wish that you feel lighter and more hopeful, even if you reached for the book more out of curiosity than struggle.

This is my true desire for you: may you truly embrace next. May you be a shiny, thriving bird in the center of a refeathered nest. Be out there in the world doing your thing, being your very best so that when your baby birds look back from wherever they have flown to, they see you thriving. They feel the happy energy you are throwing off, and it makes them feel proud, it makes them feel inspired, it makes them want to swoop back in whenever they can to check on you... and to soak up your energy!

Knowing they'll find you happy when they return is a precious thing. I know because it's how I find my mother, though I have to check in ahead of time. Even in retirement, she's refeathered: teaching part time, volunteering, and staying active in many social circles, and I'm happy that she's enjoying her life.

As for my Gram, well, she didn't drive, so that made it really easy to pin her down. I lived my life until 40 knowing she was in her cozy little house and that when I showed up, I'd find her cheerfully content and ready to make me feel like the star of the show. I'm not sure what the empty nest transition was like for her, but for as long as I can remember, she was in a refeathered nest and setting a wonderful example to live by.

Deliberately project contentment outward. It's attractive to everyone, including your young adult children. You don't need them to validate your empty nest transition, and you shouldn't let them dictate the way that emotional process unfolds. But be aware that they'll be watching to see how and when you move forward.

If there's a phase when they choose to do their own thing and they don't seem to be paying attention, they don't seem to want to visit, you have to allow that too. You have to give them their space and trust that they're out there learning and growing. Their journey was woven up with yours for as long as it needed to be, and if it's meant to be, it will be again.

Master your refeathered flow and make sure they know where to find you.

Trust.

Believe.

Enjoy :)

Additional Reading & Resources
that supported my empty nest journey

A Year of Yes by Shonda Rhimes

You are the One by Kute Blackson

The Big Leap by Dr. Gay Hendricks

Present Over Perfect by Shauna Niequist

Big Magic: Creative Living Beyond Fear by Elizabeth Gilbert

The Choice: Embrace the Possible by Dr. Edith Eva Eger

Headspace, the meditation app

The Unbelievable Freedom Habit Guide Series

If you enjoyed this book and would like to continue your
Unbelievable Freedom journey, there are other titles to collect!

Fasting Feasting Freedom: A 33 Day Habit Creation Guide by Kim Smith

Poster Girl Habits: Creating an Intentional Contentment Practice by Kim Smith

A Superhero You: Activate Your Unstoppable Powers by Barbara Anne Cookson

And coming soon...

Script Your Life: A Guide to Lasting Change Creation by Tam Veilleux

Information about all of these workbook-style Habit Guides
can be found at www.unbelievablefreedom.com,
along with links to their Amazon listings.

Believe in Unbelievable Freedom

Enjoy Your Life!

Made in the USA
Lexington, KY
07 December 2019